YOU CAN PLAY GOLF FOREVER

YOU CAN PLAY
GOLF FOREVER

PAUL L. HEXTER

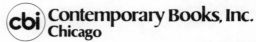 Contemporary Books, Inc.
Chicago

Library of Congress Cataloging in Publication Data

Hexter, Paul Louis, 1904—
    You can play golf forever.

    Bibliography: p.
    Includes index.
    1. Golf. 2. Aged—Recreation. 3. Nutrition.
I. Title
GV965.H45   796.352   78-73668
ISBN 0-8092-7364-0
ISBN 0-8092-7363-2 pbk.

Illustrations by George Kraynak

Published by Contemporary Books, Inc.
180 North Michigan Avenue, Chicago, Illinois 60601
Manufactured in the United States of America
Library of Congress Catalog Card Number: 78-73668
International Standard Book Number: 0-8092-7364-0 (cloth)
                      0-8092-7363-2 (paper)

Published simultaneously in Canada by
Beaverbooks
953 Dillingham Road
Pickering, Ontario L1W 1Z7
Canada

Contents

Introduction

The Aging Process— How It Affects Your Golf Game and What You Can Do about It

There are two reasons for my writing this book. The first is the repayment of a debt of gratitude to the game of golf for adding so much enjoyment to my life, both in playing the game and, far more, for the many friendships I have made through it over the years.

The second is the hope that the "body wisdom" and other information I've supplied, which has worked so well for me, will enable other senior golfers to enjoy better golf for a longer time than they normally would expect, given the gradual deterioration that comes to all of us with age.

I have been involved with golf for many years, both in playing the game and on the executive side. I was Sectional Affairs Committeeman of the United States Golf Association for Florida for more than ten years. I served as President of the Miami Amateur Golf Association and am still a director. I was a Director of the Florida State Golf Association and a member of the Florida Seniors Golf Association.

Over the years I have been a pupil of golf's greatest. Since 1955, I've taken lessons at one time or another from Sam Snead, Cary Middlecoff, Tommy Armour, Harry Bradshaw, Chi Chi Rodriguez, and Bob Toski. Through their instruction and my own experience, I've gained a solid foundation in the fundamentals of this great game.

This book represents my many years of intimacy with golf, more than fifty, and since 1965 my accumulation of knowledge about senior golfing in particular. I have also conducted extensive research into the problems and theories of aging. Some of the published material that was especially helpful to me, and that I recommend to you, appears in a reading list at the back of this book.

The Three Keys to Successful Golf for Seniors

There are, in my view, three vital keys to good golf for seniors. One is the stretching and strengthening of particular muscle groups used in the golf swing. The second is improving one's internal cellular environment with an abundant supply of those essential nutrients that can delay the process of aging. And the third is adjusting your swing to the changing conditions of your body.

We are all brought into this world with a pre-programmed genetic aging pattern. Given our present knowledge, this process is not reversible. However, it is within our capabilities to mitigate some characteristics of aging and play better golf at the same time. We can go along in life passively accepting everything (including a higher handicap) as we slowly grow older, or we can use knowledge that is now available to lower our handicap, at the same time attaining greater fulfillment in life.

Obviously, people show aging in many ways and to many different degrees. Each one of us has his own unique, individual pattern. Some of us begin to experience stiffness, loss of vision and hearing, our hair turns gray (or disappears entirely), our skin wrinkles, we feel our strength decreasing along with our muscle flexibility and sexual drive. I won't try to spell out all the things that can happen in aging. I merely wish to point out that while each individual may be free of some age symptoms, others may show up far more conspicuously.

The aging process itself is as much of an enigma to scientists today as it has always been. The medical profession simply doesn't know why our bodies have built-in obsolescence. But the one thing we do know is that aging is inevitable. A prescribed span of life runs through all living things. Many insects live only twenty-four hours. Mice live a year and a half. Dogs live about twelve or thirteen years. Horses live twenty to twenty-three years. And humans are supposed to live at least seventy years. Some people and some animals, of course, do much better than the averages. Alonzo Stagg operated a lawn mower at ninety-eight. John D. Rockefeller still gave dimes away at eighty-five. Roscoe Pound wrote a five-volume work on American law at eighty-four. And George Abbott still directs plays (and plays golf) at ninety-two!

Hereditary factors are involved to a great extent, but there is more to it. On general biological grounds, every organism must have a suitable environment or it cannot live. It follows that the more suitable the environment, the better off the organism. Body cells are no exception. They will function longer and more effectively if the cells are provided with an environment best suited to their needs.

It is generally agreed that in aging, the cells and tissues of the body are impaired to a lesser or greater degree. Probably some of these conditions are partly due to a poorer blood supply. Your blood *quality* can be lowered, for example, by inadequacies in the diet, whereas your blood *quantity* can be reduced simply by the vessels becoming less efficient. Both conditions can be helped to some degree by supplementary nutrition and proper exercise.

I hope that, after reading this book, you will take advantage of the tremendous amount of research that has been done during the past decade in the fields of physical fitness and nutrition, and that you will use it as I have for the great satisfaction that comes from continuing to play the game well.

For most of us, our life-styles have been sedentary, and while we do get some exercise playing golf and just moving around, this is not enough to keep our reflexes sharp. For one to play good golf, the muscles involved must be fully extended. The first part of my program, therefore, is a series of muscle stretches that are easy to do, take little time, and will give you much better golfing performance. They will also bring more feel into your game.

Most of us give too little thought to what we eat, so long as the quantity and quality satisfy us. Here again, by acting on the conclusions of modern research in nutrition, we can improve our golfing performance as well as retard the aging process. That's the second part of my program.

Finally, as we age, our body measurements change. Both men and women lose about an inch of height between ages thirty-nine and fifty-nine. Men lose another inch between ages fifty-nine and sixty-nine, while women lose another half inch. No matter what we do, our reflexes are not as good as they used to be.

Therefore, adjustments must be made in your swing to compensate for these constant factors in aging. The swing changes I advocate are not difficult, but if you want to continue playing well, they must be made.

Follow my three-part rehabilitation program and your senior golfing problems will be well on their way to being solved. I guarantee it. Besides, you have nothing to lose. It can't make you worse, but it might make you a whole lot better!

TABLE 1. LOSS OF HEIGHT WITH AGE

AGE	MEN	WOMEN
39-44	½"	¼"
44-49	¼"	⅛"
49-54	¼"	¼"
54-59	⅛"	¼"
59-64	½"	¼"
64-69	⅝"	¼"

TOTAL HEIGHT LOSS (30 YEARS):

2¼"	1⅜"

Above measurements taken from a population of 27,515 males and 33,562 females.

Source: *Social Survey*, p. 163, Table 1 (London: 1950).

Note: While most people realize that older people have some height loss, they are unaware that it starts in the late thirties and continues progressively. These are the averages for a large number of people. You as an individual may lose more or less than these averages, but lose height you will.

YOU CAN PLAY
GOLF FOREVER

1

How I Lost My Golf Game— and Found It Again

Back in 1965, at sixty years of age, I became a real basket case. Ever since I'd graduated from college, golf had been one of my greatest joys. I loved the game with a passion, and I'd become pretty good at it, too. I was always on the team representing our club in inter-city matches, varying between a two and six handicap.

But suddenly—it seems in retrospect as though it happened overnight—I couldn't do anything right. Putting was the worst. At times I would lose all coordination. I'd hit a three-footer three feet beyond the hole. I had an almost irresistible urge to hit the putt before I finished the backswing. I knew what was happening and spent hours on the practice green trying to correct it. I'd finish each practice session perfectly satisfied, but as soon as I got out on the course I'd completely lose control. I'd hit too long on a short putt, come up halfway on a long one.

I was like the golfer who had a two-foot

putt for a win on the eighteenth hole and left it short. His partner asked, "Why didn't you hit it harder?" And he replied, "I hit it as hard as I could!" That's how bad I was.

Much of the pleasure of golf comes from playing well at any age. It's the one game we can all play and have fun at, even into our eighties. George Abbott, dean of Broadway playwrights, never took up the game until he was seventy-two. Now, at ninety-two, he plays a remarkable game in the low nineties. He even gets into the eighties once in a while. We played together in an LPGA Pro-Am several years ago, and he distinguished himself by having three natural deuces on the short holes. Our pro teammate, Debbie Austin, was so ecstatic she gave him a big kiss.

But nothing is more frustrating than a reasonably good golfer who becomes a senior and begins that long downhill slide. In my own case, I knew subconsciously that age had something to do with it, but I didn't think or

1

feel much different than when I was twenty years younger.

Anyway, I decided to try to do something about it. In 1965, I had bought a horse farm in Ireland. It might seem strange to talk about horses in connection with a senior trying to get his golf game back, but if it had not been for my farm this story could never have been told. There was lots of land on that farm, and I reasoned that if I put in a golf green on the front lawn—far enough away from the house so a shank wouldn't break any windows—I might at least be able to work on my short game.

It was a lovely dream. I built the green and for about a year I hit at least 150 iron shots almost every day. There was some improvement at first, although nothing like what I was looking for. I experimented with everything I could think of and reviewed piecemeal all the fundamentals, but nothing much seemed to help.

Then one day my neck felt stiff. I tried rubbing and stretching it to get the kinks out. After losing some of the stiffness, I resumed my practice, but the next day I had the same problem. It dawned on me that every time I took my backswing that little kink in my neck caused my upper shoulders to tighten up so I couldn't swing fully.

That was the beginning of the sober truth that most of us who have led a comparatively sedentary life must eventually come to grips with. Our physical capabilities have gradually diminished over the years simply because we have done nothing actively to preserve them. But even if we were strong-minded enough to walk four miles or jog for half an hour a day, the usual recommendation for physical fitness, it would have no beneficial effect on one's golf game—*because most of the muscles used in golf do not come into play during these activities.*

I began to experiment with muscle stretching and discovered this can have a marvelous effect on your golf game—regardless of age or the fact that you haven't fully flexed those muscles for years. I also discovered that, as a senior, you can do more to improve your golf game on your bedroom floor than you ever can

on the practice tee. I guarantee that just spending a few minutes daily on body alignment and stretching, using the simple program I've outlined in the following pages, can be far more productive than spending several hours hitting balls off the practice tee.

The more you follow this routine of alignment and stretching, the more you will be convinced of its necessity. The time required is very little—seven to ten minutes a day. No great effort is involved. After all, you are not trying to look like Mr. America. What you are trying to do is apply daily lubrication to your chassis, giving yourself a tuneup that will enhance your golf performance.

The usual setting-up exercises and calisthenics have one thing in common: They are boring. Most of us at one time or another—usually on New Year's Day—have made resolutions to keep more fit during the coming year. My own self-promises usually lasted a week. Alignment and stretching, however, are completely different approaches, because they tie into a goal achievement that is measurable on the golf course. And it is never boring to play better golf!

Stiffness is one of the symptoms of aging. Its onset is so gradual and subtle that most of us do not realize it is happening. We may find it a little more difficult to get out of an automobile after driving an hour, but we pay no attention. Besides, you would hardly trouble yourself with an exercise routine just so you could be more agile about getting out of automobiles. Back problems also plague most of us at some time. I have thrown my back out bending over to tie my shoes. I have also done it with a misstep on a golf course. The routines I have devised for golf, while not specifically designed for that purpose, can strengthen your sacroiliac and do away with further back problems.

Your body has its own natural alignment. Young and active, you can assume a relaxed position and all your muscle groups move freely without any hitches or kinks. Everything works smoothly and aligns itself properly. But as you get older and lead a more sedentary existence, those little-used muscle groups can no longer be fully extended without spasm. By spasm I mean the burning or stinging sensation you feel when a little-used muscle is suddenly overextended.

When you were younger, your joints were well lubricated by synovial fluid. As your body wears out, these fluids are not manufactured as readily, and your movements are not as free as they once were. You can compensate for this by lying flat on the floor and moving various joints, muscles, and ligaments so that they assume their normal relationship and alignment.

To give yourself a simple demonstration, lie down on your back, flat on the floor, relaxed. Then, with your hand on your chin, push your head first to the right and then to the left, alternately touching both shoulders with your chin. If you can touch each shoulder without static or spasm, you don't need a rehabilitation program. Your body alignment is good, your joints are well lubricated, and everything is in its proper place. However, if you cannot touch your shoulders easily, if the exercise stings and there's a lot of static, it indicates the poor condition not only of your neck but also the rest of your body.

In your grandfather's time, every athletic team coach knew a "bone setter" to whom he sent players for sprains, spasms, ligament troubles, and sacroiliac problems. The "bone setter" would give gentle but increasingly firm massage and gradually manipulate the injured part back to its natural alignment. This was the basis for the development of what later came to be known as osteopathy.

Some years ago, it was heretical for a medical doctor to recommend an osteopath for lower-back trouble. Bed rest and a hot-water bottle were the standard prescriptions. But many people knew from local lore that a quicker way to recovery was through an osteopath.

Osteopathy, founded in the 1890's, held that the underlying cause of disease was structural derangement. Therapy was based on the removal of the derangement by specific manipulation. Massage was used to relax the muscles surrounding the derangement, and the problem area was pressed back into its natural alignment.

In many cases of back strain and sciatic problems osteopathy remains the quickest way to relief. Today it is a recognized part of medical practice, and I recommend it as a possible alternative when you are unable to correct a situation through your own efforts. Generally speaking, however, if you are willing to devote a few minutes a day to a series of stretching exercises, you will not only improve your golf game, you will help your body align itself naturally, probably ridding yourself of back problems as well.

The necessity for proper body alignment becomes increasingly greater as the years go by. If the lower back muscles are flexed daily, and the joints are moved about so they are freely lubricated, there is far less danger of throwing your back out. Daily alignment is a do-it-yourself treatment that pays excellent dividends.

Don't harbor the delusion that, just because you are still playing golf and feel no muscle spasms, all of your muscle groups are in good condition. Once you start the stretching and alignment program, you will find out how self-deceptive that thought can be.

In my exercise program, the entire body is stretched in a way directly related to what goes on in a golf swing. When you swing a golf club, the head remains still and the shoulders turn 90° on the backswing and then 180° from there to the completion of your follow-through. These turns should be without any restriction. When I first tried turning this way without a club, I could only turn to the left halfway. Turning farther caused muscle spasm and discomfort. Obviously, a free and easy finish in my golf swing was physically impossible.

I always knew I was not finishing the way I should, but I assumed it was some flaw in swing mechanics. It never occurred to me until then that it was due to a physical inability to make the complete shoulder turn. I was never conscious of any pain because, unconsciously, I never turned far enough to cause the pain.

To grasp the relationship between the recommended stretching positions and your golf swing, forget that the hands and arms have

Figure 1.

anything to do with the swing. Visualize the head of the golfer as a small box connected to a narrow, rectangular box (the shoulders) with both rotating around the same axis, the neck.

Figure 1 represents the head and shoulders aligned as they would be when you stand to the ball at address.

Figure 2.

When you make your backswing, your head is still to the front, but your shoulders should have turned almost 90°, as in figure 2.

Figure 3.

Figure 3 represents the shoulders turned to the left at the finish of the swing. They turn 180° from the end of the backswing and 90° from the address position. This shoulder rotation occurs whenever you swing a golf club.

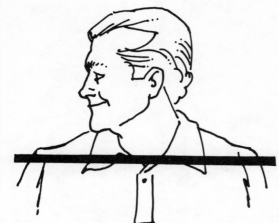

Figure 4.

Now keep the shoulders still and turn the head to the right as far as it will go, as in figure 4.

Figure 5.

Then, shoulders still, turn the head to the left as far as it will go, as in figure 5.

Compare figures 2 and 3 with figures 4 and 5. The same muscles are used in stretching, whether the shoulders turn and the head is still, or the head is turned and the shoulders are still.

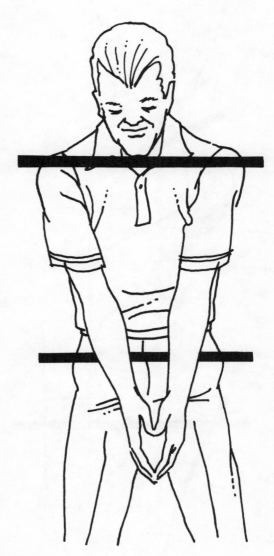

Figure 6.

Next, consider the torso area. At address, the shoulders and hips are parallel, as in figure 6.

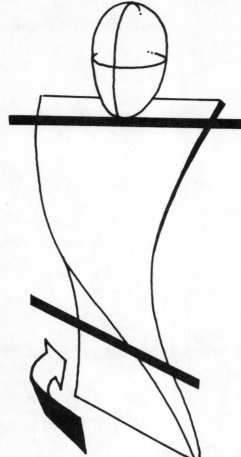

Figure 7.

Figure 8.

The torso area is stretched by keeping the shoulders still and turning the hips 45° as in figure 7, then swinging them 90°, as in figure 8.

The torso, power base of your golf swing, is where the mass of your body is concentrated. Stretching must enable both the shoulder and hip muscles to turn 180° and 90° respectively so they can take full advantage of your power base.

Figure 9.

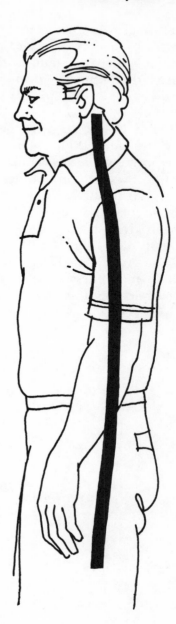

Figure 10.

Another important area is the spinal column. The greater the flexibility of your backbone, the easier it is to get the full power in your swing. Figure 9 represents the curved backbone of the average senior golfer whose occupation is sedentary. The spinal column is malleable; its curvature is not a permanent condition. Over a period of time stretching and alignment can smooth out a lot of this curvature. The ideal, of course, is no curvature at all, but this is not attainable. However, curvature can be gradually reduced to look more like figure 10.

Anyone can pull in his stomach, stick out his buttocks, and bend his knees a little to attain a better stance at the ball. But try it without a golf club, with your arms hanging from your shoulders. How long can you hold the position? When I first tried it, I could barely hold it beyond a slow count of ten. I could feel the strain in my back muscles, but by faithfully doing the stretching exercises I was soon able to double the holding time. Today I can hold this position all day if necessary.

As your spinal column becomes more flexible, it will, by its own accord, assume a straighter line when you stand to the ball. As this happens, the buttocks will naturally protrude a little more, until gradually your swing improves.

I once asked Louise Suggs, when she was the star of the ladies' tour, what was uppermost in her mind when she swung a golf club. Her answer was, "Smoothness, always smoothness." At the time, I was not sure that I understood her, but I do now. When the torso controls the swing, the swing will be smooth. It's like that old song, "It Don't Mean A Thing If You Ain't Got That Swing." For a senior, that smoothness can only come by doing the stretching and alignment exercises daily.

The answer to a full, smooth swing with proper timing is not counting or pausing or thinking of a Viennese waltz. The answer lies in working out your body alignment, stretching out on your bedroom floor, so when those muscles tighten you can do something about it. When the stretching routine I recommend becomes as much a part of your daily routine as brushing your teeth, you will instantly know after you make a bad shot just which group of muscles tensed when they should have been relaxed.

We all know when we make a bad shot that the beast within us has taken over. After you master the routine stretches outlined in the next chapter, when the beast takes over you will recognize him at once and be able to look him straight in the eye.

2

My "Sweet Sixteen" Stretching Program

If you are a senior who has lost the secret of good golf, this is the program that can put you back in business. Once you start, progress will come quickly and you will enjoy golf more than ever. At most, the exercises will take ten minutes a day. You will probably stay with them because your basic motivation—to play better golf—is being satisfied. Moreover, you won't be tempted to backslide, because as soon as you stop for a few days it will inevitably show up on the golf course. There is nothing like coming off the ball to put you on your back on the bedroom floor!

Here is another point about these stretching routines. When we seniors have been forced away from golf for several weeks or months because of seasonal changes or business pressures, we usually ask for a couple of extra shots after we've returned to the game. If you follow these routines daily, you may still ask for the shots after a layoff—though you won't need them nearly as much. A few swings and you'll be about as good as if you'd played yesterday.

My program consists of sixteen stretching positions. During the first week, you should familiarize yourself with the positions and think about what you are trying to do with each. Some positions and some stretches will seem extremely awkward. Work on them until they become relatively easy.

Keep the book with you until you memorize all the positions. Improvement comes more rapidly than you believe. It is not necessary to push yourself. When beginning, just work on getting rid of the awkwardness, and don't worry if you can't do the suggested number.

While all sixteen positions are important, I believe the sit-ups described are basic to any good golf swing. Yet when I first tried them—I hadn't done any in years—it was all I could do to make two. It was not long, however, before I was up to ten. Then it became twenty, and on to one hundred in groups of twenty. This, too, became easy.

These exercises, when you get used to them, are simple. You will reach a plateau where you can run through them almost without thinking. That's the goal. When you can do them all easily, you'll be as agile as nature permits. Remember, doing them *more* times than the suggested number has a zero payoff.

Exercise 1—The Back Alignment Position

Lie flat on the floor with knees raised to a 45° angle, arms at your sides. Inhale fully; exhale slowly and completely. Do this five times. Then press your backbone flat against the floor, holding it there for a slow count of five. Repeat this ten times.

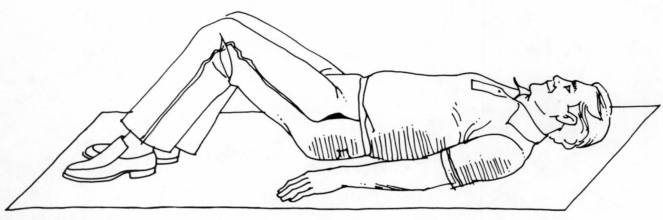

Figure 11. Exercise 1

Exercise 2—Freeing the Stomach Muscles

Place a heavy telephone book or a dictionary on your stomach. Hold it there with both hands and lift the book with your belly muscles fifty times. The heavier the book, the more good it will do. Keep your backbone pressed against the floor.

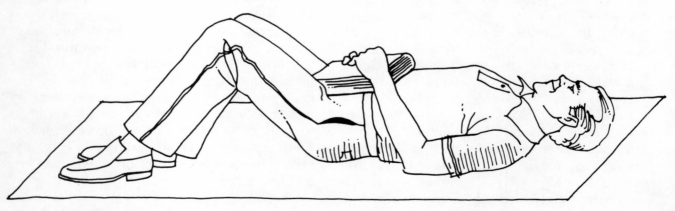

Figure 12. Exercise 2

Exercise 3—The Forward Head Press

Clasp your hands behind your head and push your head to your chest. Keep your backbone pressed against the floor. Repeat ten times. This position and the ones following are designed to free the head, neck, and shoulders.

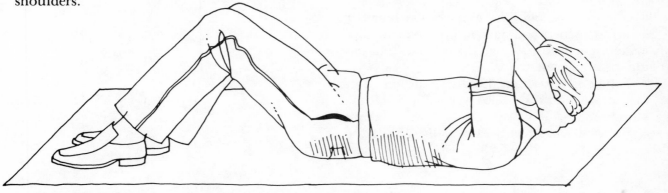

Figure 13. Exercise 3

Exercise 4—The Backward Head Press

This is similar to exercise 3, except you raise your head and, hands cupped under your chin, push it *backward* until it touches the floor. Repeat ten times.

When you do head and neck stretches, you may hear noises caused by bones rubbing against one another. You may also hear small bones clicking and snapping into place. This is what I mean by the natural alignment of the body. You can sometimes actually hear and feel your vertebrae move as you stretch yourself. It means that tight muscles have relaxed and pulled the vertebrae or other bones back in place. The more you do these exercises, the less noise you will hear. But there may always be some.

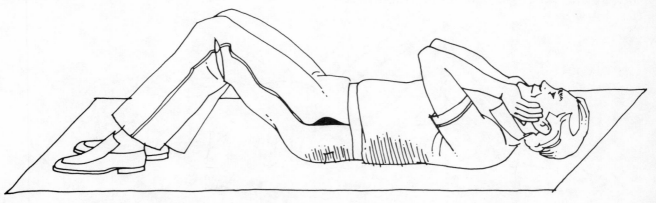

Figure 14. Exercise 4

Exercise 5—The Sideways Head Press

With your left hand against your chin, force the chin to the right until it touches the shoulder. Your head may not turn a full 90° before the muscles tighten and begin to hurt. There will be a gradual improvement in turning ability as you repeat the exercise each day. Eventually you will be able to touch either shoulder, which you have to do or you cannot make a good golf swing. Do this ten times to the right and left.

If there is restriction, hold your head still in the far position for a few counts and see if the muscle gives. It often does. However, don't strain. Your head will eventually go all the way.

Figure 15. Exercise 5

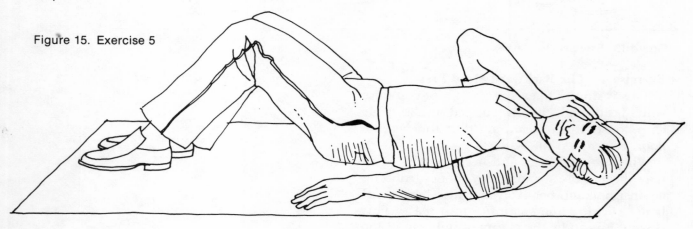

Exercise 6—The Shoulder Raise

Raise the left shoulder as high as it will go, lowering the right shoulder at the same time. Then raise the right shoulder as far as it will go, lowering the left. Do this ten times for each side. This is where I still hear the snap, crackle, and pop, even after doing these exercises for years.

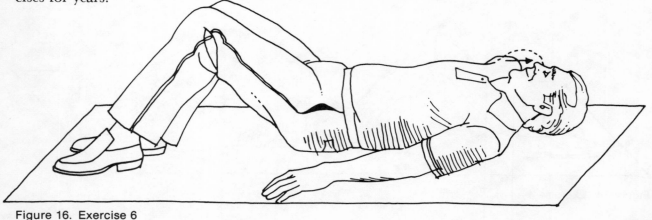

Figure 16. Exercise 6

Exercise 7—The Knee-to-Chest Pull

Grasp the left knee with both hands and bring it to your chest, pulling it as far as it will go. Do this ten times with each knee. If you feel discomfort in the lower back, alternate knees until there is no stiffness or restriction.

This exercise is a good way to relieve stiffness and muscle spasm in the lower back. The count of ten is not mandatory. It may take twenty times on certain days, but do get the stiffness worked out.

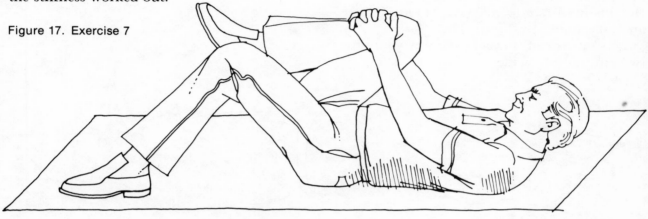

Figure 17. Exercise 7

Exercise 8—The Leg Spread

Start with the knees at the usual 45° angle from the floor, with knees and feet together, and arms at your sides. With the feet still together, spread the knees as far apart as you can, then bring them back together. Do this ten times.

This exercise stretches the inside muscles of your legs and thighs. You will likely feel some soreness because these muscles are little used except in golf.

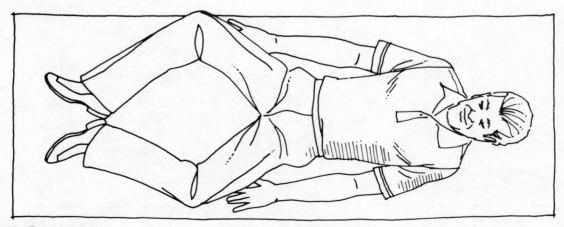

Figure 18. Exercise 8

Exercise 9—The Waist Turn

Raise your arms and grasp the left elbow with the right hand and the right elbow with the left hand. Keep your knees together.

Now swing your arms to the right and twist your waist to the left so that the left knee touches the floor on your left side and the right upper arm touches the floor on your right side. Then twist everything in reverse. You will not be able to touch the floor with your knees when you start, but as you keep at it, you will soon get limber enough to do it. Do this ten times to each side, more if there are restrictions.

This movement is exactly the way your hips twist in the golf swing.

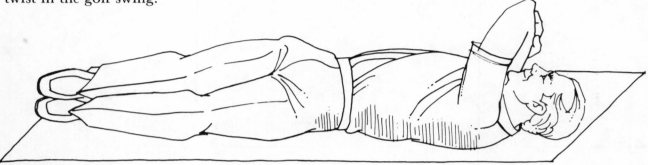

Figure 19. Exercise 9

Exercise 10—The Elbow-to-Knee Press

Clasp your hands behind your head, raise the left knee, and touch it with both elbows. Repeat ten times. Then raise the right knee and do the same. Then raise both knees and touch with both elbows ten times. I usually have to rest for a minute or so at this point.

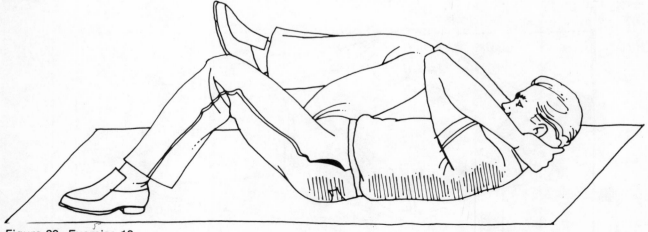

Figure 20. Exercise 10

Exercise 11—Sit-Ups

Lie flat on the floor with the legs stretched out. Hook your feet under the edge of a bed or chair for support. Arms at your sides, do twenty sit-ups.

This will be difficult to do at first, one or two may be all you can manage. Don't try to overdo it. Work up to ten gradually, then twenty. When I first started, I could do only two, but it didn't take long before I was doing twenty. You will be amazed how quickly your torso muscles strengthen.

1. When you are able to do twenty sit-ups, give yourself a rest and then do twenty more. See if you can work up to one hundred in groups of twenty. This may take two months, but it's worth it.

2. When you reach one hundred, you are ready for the next step, doing the sit-ups without support for the feet. This again will be very difficult when you first try it, but you will soon be able to do twenty without the support for your feet as easily as you did the first twenty with support.

3. When you reach this stage, add another group of twenty and touch your toes with your hands on each sit-up. This will stretch your hamstring muscles. Do this with as little knee bend as possible. You will be amazed at how quickly you progress and how easy it all becomes.

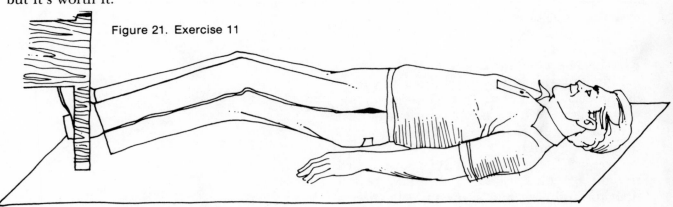

Figure 21. Exercise 11

Exercise 12—Push-Ups with a Difference

The push-up is a standard exercise that starts from a face-down prone position on the floor with hands flat on the floor next to your chest. At first, probably one or two will be all you can do, but gradually work yourself up to ten.

After you can do ten push-ups easily, hold the up position to a count of six before you let yourself down. While in this holding position, try to relax your arms at the elbows. You need to strengthen your elbow muscles so they don't tighten too soon when swinging a golf club. This problem plagues many seniors.

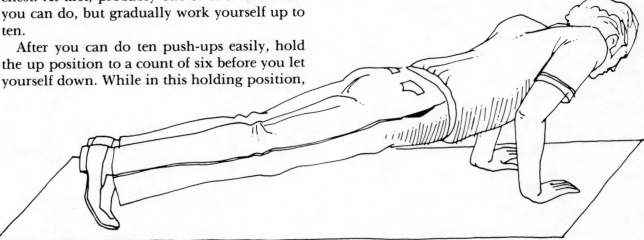

Figure 22. Exercise 12

Exercise 13—Side Push-Ups

When you are able to do ten regular push-ups, add this one. With the left palm in the regular position, but with the right forearm under your chest, do the push-up with your left arm and right shoulder only. Do this ten times, then switch to the opposite side.

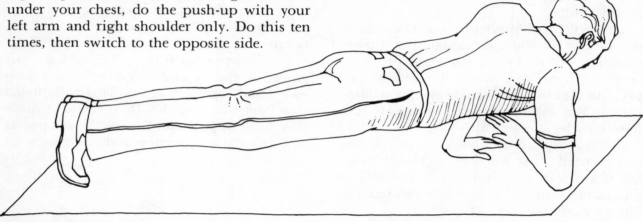

Figure 23. Exercise 13

Exercise 14—The Full Leg Stretch

I'll admit, this exercise is difficult to get set up properly and seems very awkward at the start. Begin with the usual position, flat on your back, but with the legs at a little less than the usual 45° angle.

Place the right leg fully outstretched straight over the left kneecap. Press downward with the right leg and allow the left knee to touch the floor. Keep your shoulders flat on the floor. Do this ten times with the right leg, then reverse it. Again, this exercise must be worked up to slowly, but it will come. Don't force it.

Once you have mastered this stretch, you will find it useful anytime you have a backache. It is almost the same movement that an osteopath uses to move your lumbars.

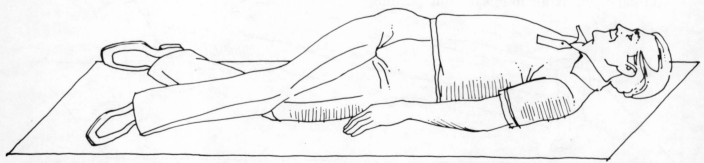

Figure 24. Exercise 14

Exercise 15—Half Squats

Stand erect with your hands on your hips and your legs in your normal golf stance. Do a half squat, bringing your knees together and keeping your feet flat on the floor. This exercise will stretch the inside muscles of your thighs and legs, so important in the golf swing.

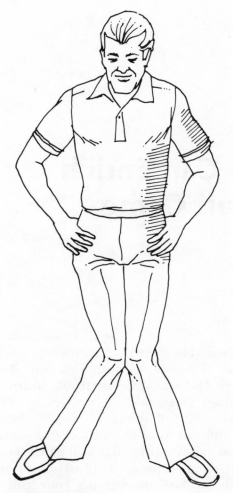

Figure 25. Exercise 15

Exercise 16—The Hand Squeeze

In the standing position, extend the fingers of both hands as far as possible. Then make a tight fist. Do this twenty times. Your hands get stiff, too, as you grow older, and this exercise will restore sensitivity, which is so vital in golf.

The reason for the great emphasis on sit-ups in these exercises is because the mass of the torso is similar to a fly wheel. As the torso turns, its force flows to the club head through levers—the upper arm, the forearm, and the club shaft. As the torso turns, the various levers make a straight line at impact and increase the speed of the club head to more than one hundred miles per hour.

The torso is the power base of the golf swing. The whole lever system will go out of whack if the hands quicken in relation to the shoulders. It is the most natural thing in the world to want to use the hands to control the speed of the swing, but it is wrong to do so. With these exercises, you will be able to slow it all down so you can get the torso in control.

In doing these exercise routines, remember that slow is always better than fast. Don't force at the beginning stages. You are the best judge of how many times to do each of these stretches. Tomorrow is another day. It took years to get yourself in the shape you are in, and you can't reverse the process overnight. Be patient. You are—or should be—past the age of being a hero, even to yourself.

Once you have the routines mastered, days will come when muscle spasms return for no apparent reason. You may get a stiff neck from being in an air-conditioned room, or you may get a crick in your back just from bending over. When something like this crops up, you can usually work out the spasm or stiffness first on one side, then the other.

If the spasm is in the lower back, for example, use exercise 7 (the knee-to-chest press). And always work both sides of the body, not just the side where you feel it. Often, working the side opposite the spasm provides the necessary relief.

3

How Good Nutrition Can Enrich and Improve Your Golf Game

There's another aspect of my recovery program for seniors that I consider just as important as my stretching program. It, too, was discovered through my involvement with raising horses on a stud farm. The manager of my farm was familiar with the use of vitamin E for horses and had begun a vitamin program at my farm. The results were so good that my interest in nutrition was greatly stimulated.

About the same time, I read somewhere that vitamin C was useful in controlling allergies. Because I was then a victim of severe hay fever, I began using vitamin C with some success. The first year I still required cortisone for maximum relief, but by the following year my hay fever was more under control. I had taken vitamin C before the first symptoms appeared and controlled it thereafter with continuing doses and antihistamines. I haven't had a shot of cortisone since.

Soon afterward, I began reading everything I could get my hands on about vitamins and nutrition. How much, I wondered, could nutrition influence performance on the golf course? And was there anything, nutritionally speaking, that could be of value in relieving the symptoms of aging?

It's difficult to accept the fact that something you eat can improve your golf game. For some it may seem an unconventional point of view. But in the last analysis it's your golf game, and the only way you can find out if nutrition is the answer is to give it a trial.

In my own case, good nutrition improved not only my golf game but also my health. For example, an ophthalmologist once told me that I had incipient cataracts that would be operable in three to four years. About a year later, on reexamination by the same doctor, the cataracts had disappeared. Surgery was not necessary. Thus, in my case at least, one of the common symptoms of aging had been retarded. This phenomenon is covered fully in Dr. Irwin Stone's *The Healing Factor*, also in

Dr. Roger Williams's *Nutrition Against Disease.*

Around this time, I had prostate trouble, hardly unusual for anyone my age. I was told that the urinary passage would eventually block completely, requiring surgery. This also has not happened, and I have no prostate problem as of today. Again, a symptom of aging had been retarded, and I can attribute it only to this program.

I also had a heart attack in 1962 that left me with attacks of fibrillation, a skipped beat, and palpitations. Although I was on the usual medications for this condition, they gradually lost their effectiveness, so I turned to daily doses of vitamins C and E. Today, I take no medication. I do not fibrillate and have no skipped beats or palpitations. The literature is full of controversy on the effectiveness of vitamin E in heart conditions. I want no part of the controversy, but I won't discontinue taking vitamins E and C under any circumstances. The doctors argue about it, but it is the patients who suffer.

What We Know about Nutrition

Knowledge about nutrition is expanding at an extremely rapid rate. About ten thousand research papers on the subject are published annually, many challenging conventional beliefs. All of us have a certain amount of body wisdom, some of it instinctive, some of it learned from personal experience. If raw onions disagree with you, you avoid them. If coffee keeps you awake, you avoid drinking it before bedtime. We instinctively choose a variety of foods for our diet, because we know that variety is better for us than eating the same foods day in, day out. We don't ask others what we should eat; we make our own decision.

Biochemists have identified some forty essential nutrients not manufactured in our own bodies which, therefore, must be ingested for survival. These substances are proteins, fats, carbohydrates, vitamins, and minerals. The proteins divide into amino acids, eight of them essential. Only one fat, linoleic acid, is considered a must. Vitamins are also essential,

as are minerals. All these substances are found in our diet, and we instinctively vary it to straddle the field and try to take in everything we need.

With the development of intensive cultivation and the bulk processing of so much of our food supply, a few consumer groups have advocated that we return to the production methods of our forefathers. This would mean abandonment of intensive nitrogen fertilization, modern fungicides, and insecticides. They argue that modern methods eliminate or diminish the amounts of essential nutrients in our food. Moreover, they claim that the artificial preservatives that have been added to preserve the shelf life of many mass-distributed foods are contaminants.

Without getting into the arguments about what contaminates and how to prevent spoilage, our return to food growing as it used to be one hundred years ago would cause starvation in the world on a much larger scale than is now present.

White flour is the usual example given of a food degraded by processing. The modern milling process developed about 100 years ago does destroy some essential nutrients. The Food and Drug Administration, however, requires white-bread manufacturers to replace many of the lost nutrients, so we really are not as nutritionally mistreated as some would like us to believe. Otherwise, the United States could not be the granary for 50 percent of the world population.

On the other hand, the Food and Nutrition Board of the National Research Council regularly issues a statement concerning the proper amounts of vitamins and minerals necessary to fulfill one's minimum daily requirements, or RDA (Recommended Dietary Allowance), and thus insure the maintenance of good health. These minimums do *not* take into consideration the losses in nutritional value that result from food storage, processing, and preparation, which can amount to an aggregate loss of as much as 50 percent or more of the vitamins you take in.

It is also well known that the levels of certain vitamins and minerals in older people are well below the levels deemed essential for the maintenance of good health. Just as the FDA requires nutrient replacement in white flour to insure minimal vitamins and minerals in your diet, it makes good common body sense to supplement your diet with a vitamin and mineral supplement that spans the entire spectrum. You will then be sure you are getting more than the recommended minimum.

Vitamin C

The story of vitamin C, ascorbic acid, is an interesting one. In the eighteenth century, scurvy inevitably occurred on long sea voyages and as many as 80 percent or more of crews would be disabled. Many of the men lost their teeth, went berserk, even died. Captain Cook, whose exploration gave Great Britain so many of its island possessions in the eastern hemisphere, somehow knew that fresh fruit and even sauerkraut helped protect his sailors from scurvy.

Although this information was faithfully reported to the British admiralty, it took years before a daily ration of lime juice, rich in vitamin C, became the order of the day. Some historians believe that the superiority of the British Navy over the French in that era was directly traceable to its ability to keep its crews healthy with a daily ration of lime juice.

Vitamin C is indeed a tremendously interesting essential nutrient. Most creatures have had the ability to manufacture it. The exceptions are man, primates, and guinea pigs. Anthropologists theorize that some twenty-five million years ago so much vitamin C was available in the daily diet that human bodies did not need to manufacture it, and therefore we lost the ability to do so.

It is now universally accepted, of course, that vitamin C is an essential nutrient, and we must ingest a quantity of it daily. The RDA recommendation is forty-five milligrams a day as the minimum requirement.

As in many fields where conventionalism is being challenged, acceptance of a newer concept makes slow progress. Dr. Linus Pauling, the only living recipient of two Nobel Prizes, published a book in 1971 entitled *Vitamin C and the Common Cold,* in which he recom-

mended taking gram quantities of vitamin C daily for the maintenance of good health.

Not only is vitamin C one of the cheapest, most harmless nutrients available it is also often mentioned in connection with the aging process. Its use has been strongly recommended for those past middle age, and there are substantial reasons for believing that it is tremendously important.

For example, stiffening of the joints is commonly associated with aging—and with poorer golf performance. It has been suggested that the production of collagen, the cement that binds our cells together, takes place more readily when we are young and less so as we grow older. Since vitamin C is essential for building collagen, it seems probable that more abundant supplies of it as we grow older could slow down the deterioration of collagen production.

Other nutritional observations on rabbits, rats, and human beings who have been given large supplements of vitamin C show a decrease in arteriosclerosis, one of the usual symptoms of aging. In the same context, it is often found that the tissues and body fluids in older people are extremely low in vitamin C, indicating a much larger requirement is necessary.

Vitamin C is also a strong antioxidant, therefore preventing unwanted oxidation in the tissues and body fluids. Oxidation is a chemical process in which a molecule combines with oxygen, causing change. Rust is caused by iron combining with oxygen; rubber bands lose elasticity, dry up, and become brittle through oxidation; bread becomes stale for the same reason.

Oxidation is one of the biochemical changes associated with aging, and oxidation can be inhibited by an antioxidant, such as vitamin C, a water-soluble antioxidant. Vitamin E is also an antioxidant but is oil soluble. In fact, vitamins C and E work together synergistically, the action of one reinforcing the action of the other. Antioxidants have clearly increased the life span of rats. So while the purpose of vitamin supplementation is primarily to increase your athletic performance, it is quite possible you will get extra dividends from it. It certainly hasn't been proved that you won't.

For all practical purposes, therefore, heavy doses of Vitamin C, harmless, seem to slow up the deleterious effects of aging. It is particularly appropriate for the senior golfer who is trying to keep his golf game going as long as possible.

A number of orthopedic surgeons have determined that patients with back pains and backaches might recover more quickly if they took large (gram) quantities of vitamin C. The reports of their patients were so encouraging that today many physicians recommend daily gram quantities of vitamin C strictly as a preventive measure.

I can attest to this particular benefit of vitamin C. I had a sacroiliac back problem when I was about sixty-two, not unusual for a senior golfer. But this problem was so severe I couldn't even get up or down the stairs. A corset with a steel brace and special exercises were prescribed. I was also told that if I did not get relief, I would need an operation—but the operation was successful only 50 percent of the time!

Golf, of course, was completely out. The corset did give relief, but it took months before I was free from pain. I was out of golf for more than a year but continued to wear the corset every time I got into an automobile or took an airplane. I was afraid not to. The doctor said, "Play golf only with the corset on." And I can guarantee you that the corset is not a gadget that will improve your game.

Then I read about how large quantities of vitamin C could be helpful in cases of back problems. Since vitamin C is harmless, as well as an essential food component, I felt I had nothing to lose by increasing the quantities I had been taking.

Now, whether it was the vitamin regimen or the stretching, or a combination of both, I cannot say, but today my back feels strong. It *is* strong. I can do a hundred sit-ups easily with my feet unsupported, and I am sure that if there were any point to it, I could work up to several hundred. But most important, my back has never gone out again, and I can make a full turn with no effort. I have not played in

a corset for several years, much to my comfort.

I do have back stiffness at times, but that is completely different from real back pain, which I never experience. The stiffness is easily worked out by exercising, sometimes by just lying flat on the floor.

When I say my back feels strong, I mean it. I carry my own suitcases. I walk eighteen holes if there are no carts. And while I don't like it, I still carry my golf bag on occasion. You don't do these things if your back is in bad shape, and many men in my age group would be terrified of injuring themselves. I would, too, if it were not for my program.

Fortunately, vitamin C is one of the least toxic substances known. The largest dosage on record, 180 grams, was given intravenously during a twenty-four-hour period without *any* side effects. So, for senior golfers who are subject to backache and stiffness, additional vitamin C is good body wisdom. My advice is to supplement your daily food intake with at least one gram of powdered vitamin C (¼ level teaspoonful) with an equal amount of baking soda dissolved in a glass of water morning and evening. (The baking soda makes it fizz, neutralizing the acid of vitamin C, rendering it tasteless.)

The actual amount needed can vary among individuals, according to Dr. Pauling, from two to nine grams daily. How do you find out the proper dosage for your own needs? If two grams don't help after a few weeks, increase the dosage to three grams daily, then more if necessary. Raise it gradually until you find the dosage that helps you most. Remember, vitamin C cannot harm you and will probably prevent you from having colds as well. It works that way for me, and it works that way for Dr. Pauling.

Obviously, any senior thinking about improving his golf game should try to provide the cells and tissues in his body with the most effective nutrients he can find. This will help his body minimize degenerative diseases and slow down the deterioration that comes with aging.

Vitamin E

Vitamin E is a completely harmless substance. Children have been given amounts in excess of three thousand units daily over a long period without side effects.

When the Olympics were held in Mexico City, at an altitude of eight thousand feet, a number of participants supplemented their daily food intake with an additional five hundred units or more of vitamin E. Our Olympic swimming team also trained on it. The rationale behind this program was that vitamin E, a potent antioxidant, would reduce the oxygen requirement of the body as it underwent strenuous exertion at high altitudes.

The physical fitness director at the University of Illinois, Dr. Thomas K. Cureton, has documented the use of wheat germ oil for athletes as vital to their athletic training. One of the active ingredients of wheat germ oil is vitamin E.

In Dr. Cureton's experiments, one group consisted of men older than fifty who were the usual sedentary types. In six months, their fitness, measured by several types of endurance tests, improved about 50 percent. About 20 percent of this improvement was credited to increased exercise, another 30 percent to diet supplementation.

To sum up, many people concerned about their athletic performance supplement their diets with vitamin E and feel that it plays an important part in increased physical endurance. They believe that by taking five hundred I.U.s (International Units) of vitamin E daily, they experience less fatigue and enjoy greater endurance. As senior golfers, we would be foolish to pass up any chances of increasing our staying power.

Fiber

Fiber is the crude, undigested residue left over from the food we eat. Vegetables and cereals are sources of fiber. Meat and fruits, in most cases, contain little.

In the last few years, biochemists and physicians have shown great interest in reports about certain African tribes whose daily diet contains twenty-five grams of fiber. These people apparently do not suffer from appendicitis, diverticulosis, cancer of the colon, or other diseases of the digestive tract.

Our normal diet in this country includes about 2 to 2 ½ grams of crude fiber daily. If we were to increase the daily amount of fiber to something closer to the African diet, the reasoning goes, we should be less prone to most gastrointestinal disturbances.

From earliest childhood, we've been taught that daily evacuation is desirable. Our own body wisdom agrees with this. We also know that skipping a day does not necessarily mean we are ill, but it is a sign our bodies are not functioning with peak efficiency. One of the best ways to insure regularity is by adding more fiber to your diet.

The actual amount of crude fiber essential for good health has not been determined, but it appears to be about 5½ grams daily. And the best way to attain that intake is to eat bran. Porridge is out for most seniors because of the extra calories (400 with milk and sugar). The easiest way, the one involving fewest calories, is to use a processed bran cereal: 100 % Bran, All-Bran, or Bran Buds. Cereals such as 40% Bran or Raisin Bran only provide half this amount of fiber.

Eat a serving of any of these 100% bran cereals with fat-free milk and a sugar substitute and you will add three grams of fiber to your daily diet. You are probably getting at least 2½ grams daily already, so you will then be reasonably close to the recommended amount.

By accepting these four diet recommendations—a vitamin and mineral supplement, vitamin E (500 units daily), vitamin C (in gram quantities twice daily), and fiber (3 grams daily furnished by 100% bran)—you will begin a simple health routine that will pay big dividends. The results will not come overnight, but try it for six months before making up your mind. I guarantee this program will make it easier for you to play better golf—whatever your age. It also has implications regarding aging, specifically, involving cell structure.

The basic structure of all living things is cellular. In the laboratory, cells are studied and kept alive with nutrient solutions. Such solutions can be very poor and the cells soon die, or they can be very good and the cells will divide and multiply for years, or they can be anywhere in between.

As most of us seniors are aware, we are programmed to age gradually, but only recently has aging been studied by scientists through research on the living cell. They've learned that when a cell does not reproduce itself perfectly—this is not uncommon—it gives off a free radical which combines quickly with any available molecule. Vitamin C, readily combines with free radicals and takes them out of circulation before they become harmful.

One prominent theory of aging holds that as cells grow older they tend to throw off more free radicals, no longer replicating themselves accurately. If this theory is true, then by stepping up our intake of vitamins C and E we can minimize the damage done by free radicals, thus retarding at least some of the effects of aging.

Although I have taken vitamins C and E for years, I did so not with the idea that it could minimize the effects of aging. Actually, this theory came to the fore almost ten years *after* I was on this regime. Fortunately, in my case, aging has been a gradual process and has not been accompanied by many common complaints of the elderly. This may be due to the vitamin program, the stretching routines, or both. I only know that my general health is so much better that it is hard to believe. Whereas I used to complain to the doctor constantly, I now have no real need to even seek his advice.

I'm reminded of a story about the late Al Jolson, a real hypochondriac. At lunch one day, one of Jolson's friends mentioned a new disease his doctor had just discovered.

"The symptoms," Jolson's friend explained, "are quite unusual. The patient has no real complaints—he just feels good all the time."

Jolson said, "Give me the name of that doctor. I'm sure it's what I've got."

This may seem unrelated to golf, but not when you're a senior. At our age, it's more important than ever to be in the best possible condition. And by using these routines for the improvement of your golf game, you may derive other dividends that go far beyond your favorite sport and mine.

Remember, when you have satisfied the RDA, you are only providing the minimum cellular environment required to prevent deficiency diseases. When you add large amounts of vitamins C and E, even though the excess is excreted, you are providing a more optimal cellular environment. And for most people that means a much more active life.

On the record, the largest amount of vitamin C ever taken is 180 grams over 24 hours with no ill effects. Children have been treated with 3,000 units of vitamin E daily over a period of years also with no ill effects. These are huge amounts. Like food components, they are similar to sugar and salt as far as body harm goes. So providing yourself with a more optimal cellular environment is really an update on how you, as a senior, can counter some of the effects of aging and play better golf at the same time.

4

How to Improve Your Swing with Pregame Drills and Self-Analysis

After you have followed the recommendations for stretching, body alignment, and food supplementation, allow time for them to take hold before starting to work on your golf game itself. You can hardly expect a week of stretching to smooth out muscle groups that have not been fully extended for years, nor are the effects of food supplementation evident overnight. Results come from a cumulative buildup. It would be wonderful if there were a secret to instant golf improvement, but so far no one seems to have it.

Most seniors are heavier, broader, and shorter than they were at maturity. Even if your weight hasn't changed, your measurements have. It happens to all of us. It's simply a natural redistribution that goes along with the aging process.

In my own case, I'm two inches shorter than when I was in the air corps, and I'm sure this loss in height is another contributing factor to the deterioration of my golf swing. When I held the club the same distance away from me that I always had, it still looked right and felt right. But with the loss of two inches in height, I was standing too close to the ball at address.

This is not a fatal error. No position in golf is fatal—you can hit the ball from any position—but you'll hit it better, straighter, and more often from the right position.

My inclination as a senior was to cozy up to the ball. Even today I have to frequently check my address position to make sure my arms are hanging freely from the shoulders, not drawn in slightly.

To assess what time has done to your own body measurements and to help you correct some of its damages, the following drills will be useful.

The Address Position

I think 50 percent of every golf shot is

25

determined by the way you stand to the ball and what you do before you make the swing. I suggest a method for positioning yourself which can be practiced in your bedroom. Once you can assume the correct address position and hold it easily for at least a minute, then take it out to the practice tee.

The Address Position Number 1
Stand with your back against a wall, your feet as wide apart as in your golf stance, your heels about three inches away from the wall. Press your backbone against the wall so it becomes straight. Your shoulders should now touch the wall, along with your backbone and the upper part of your buttocks. With no conscious effort, your belly automatically tucks itself up. Your arms fall loosely at your sides.

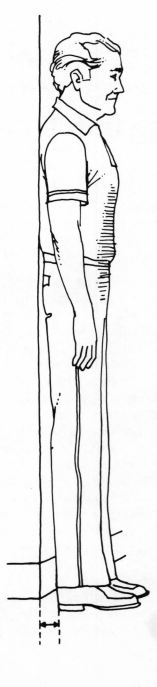

Figure 26. Address position 1

The Address Position Number 2
Hold this position and move out about a
foot from the wall, keeping the backbone as
straight as it was against the wall.

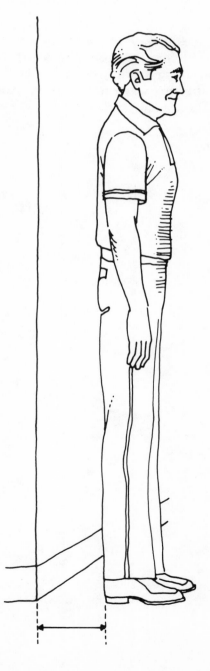

Figure 27. Address position 2

The Address Position Number 3
Now bend forward from the *waist*, letting your arms hang from your shoulders. They should hang this way on every shot, from the driver to the wedge.

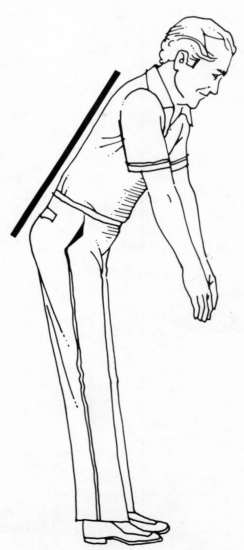

Figure 28. Address position 3

The Address Position Number 4

Release your knees. When you do this, you should feel the tension go out of your belly.

Now release your right hip. Automatically, your chin will point to the right. Bring your hands together as if you were holding a golf club. This will put you in excellent position to stand to the ball. It's like so many things in golf—if you can't do it without a club, you surely can't do it with a club.

Practice this setup position in your bedroom until it becomes second nature to you, until you feel you could stand this way all day. The straight backbone, essential to a good golf swing, is easy if you have everything loosened up by stretching. I am ashamed to admit it, but the first time I did this setup, I could hold the position only about two seconds. No wonder I became a basket case.

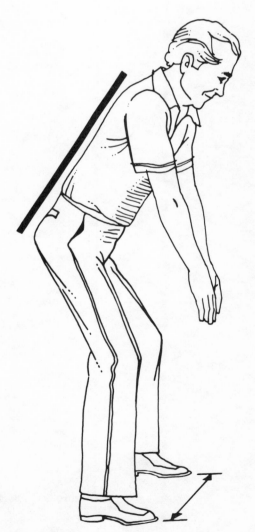

Figure 29. Address position 4

The Shoulder Turn

From the final address position, let your arms hang down at your sides and turn your shoulders to the right a full 90° as you are supposed to do on your backswing. *Your head should not move. Your right shin should not move.* Your left knee should start the turn with a move to the side, not to the front.

The first time you try this you may discover a lot of things about your turn that are hard to believe. Although you know there should be no side movement or sway, it may take some practice before you can eliminate it.

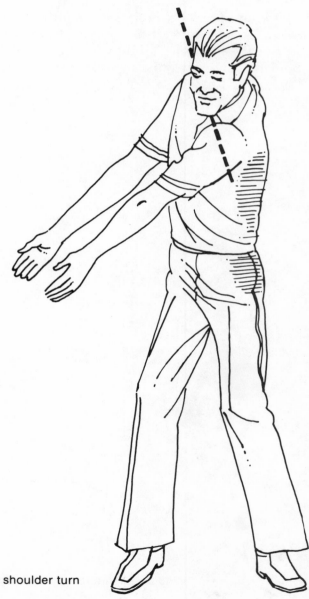

Figure 30. The shoulder turn

Beginning the Downswing

After you have mastered the shoulder turn-(but not before), it's time to practice the start of the downswing. Again, this should be done *without* a club.

First, return to the 90° shoulder position. Relax the knees. Then, keeping the head still and the shoulders set, slide your knees forward and out from under you. The upper part of your body and your head should remain still and in the same position. Slide the knees back and forth ten times, but keep your weight on the insides of both feet.

This exercise demonstrates how little violence should occur at the beginning of the downswing. It also shows how little movement actually takes place during the first and most important movement of the downswing.

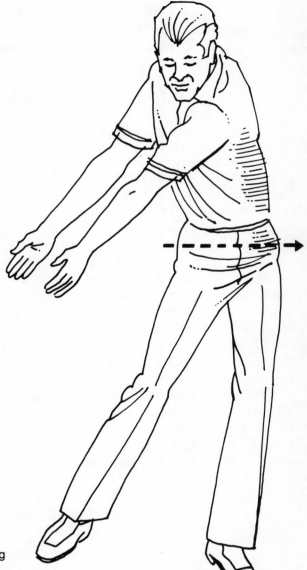

Figure 31. Beginning the downswing

A Simple Photographic Check for Swing Basics

A picture is supposed to be worth a thousand words. In golf, a few pictures can save you hours of hitting balls on the practice tee, and in this section I'm going to show how you can use a camera to your best advantage.

How often have you heard a golfer say, after hitting a clinker, "I came off the ball," "I moved my head," "I hit too soon"? A golf ball can be hit from any position with almost any grip. Paul Hahn used to demonstrate this standing on one leg, hitting with one hand, using a golf club with a rubber shaft. However, there are two fundamental positions that cannot be violated. One is the shoulder turn, the other the hip turn. I don't mean to imply that if you are correct in these two positions everything will come up roses, but your chances will sure improve.

It's that simple. If you don't have the fundamentals right, you don't stand much of a chance of improving your game. I want to show you how these two fundamental positions can be easily checked by taking a few photographs of yourself swinging a golf club. First, you need someone with a camera to take pictures of you on the practice tee from a point directly behind you. Use a tripod, or brace the camera against a tree or any stationary object, just so long as a second picture can be taken from the same point without moving the camera. Trying to hold the camera still without bracing won't work. There will always be some movement regardless of how careful you are. Also, your pictures will turn out better if the sun is directly behind you and the photographer.

Now tee up a ball and assume your normal address position. Try it with a driver first. Have the first picture taken at address, the second at the exact top of your backswing. If you're doing this on a practice tee, go ahead and actually hit the ball. Have several groups of shots taken, to make sure your photographer catches the second picture right at the top of your swing. You might try stopping your backswing at the top, having the second picture taken then. It won't be quite as good as a real swing, but if a practice tee setup is not available, it should suffice.

When you have the two prints in front of you, take the address print (see photo A) and draw a line from the ball through the middle of the top of your right shoulder to the top of the print (see photo B). Measure how far that line is from the left-hand edge of the print. Then take the print of your backswing and draw a similar line through the ball to the top of the print the same distance from the edge of the picture as the line in photo B (see photo C). If you have made a proper turn, your hands should touch, or be above, this line. If your hands are below the line, something is wrong. You are not turned enough, and you are too flat.

It is worth checking the top of your backswing with this photo sequence every few months. We seniors are inclined to go back to old ways. In my own case, photo C indicates that, while my hands are in good position, the club has not quite reached the position parallel to the ground where it should be. The answer, of course, is to take a few practice swings until the shaft is parallel. Only a fraction more turn is needed. I was probably getting lazy.

Checking Other Points

These same pictures can give you information about your own swing that is hard to come by any other way. By wearing a button-down cardigan, you can also get a good idea of the degree of hip turn. Notice how the sweater buttons act to divide your torso. At the top of the backswing (photo C), the sweater buttons indicate that the hips have turned 45°, as they should.

Now look at the angle of the club face at the top of the backswing in photo C. If it points to the sky, the face has been opened. If it is perpendicular to the ground, the face has been closed. The better position, neither open nor closed, is halfway, as shown here.

Photo A. The address position

Photo B. Address position with line drawn through ball and center of right shoulder

Photo C. Backswing position with line drawn through ball to edge of photo

Head Movement

Photos D and E feature my friend and frequent playing partner, Frank Strafaci, now a senior, who was, in the late 1930s, a nationally known amateur golfer.

Notice in the address position picture (photo D) that a line has been drawn between the ball and the left foot (AA). This is the baseline which appears in both prints because it is drawn between two fixed points, the ball and the left toe, regardless of the backswing.

At the top of the left toe, another line (BB) has been drawn perpendicular to the baseline, giving you the same reference lines in both pictures. Compare the back of the head in both pictures to the perpendicular line. It shows no head movement, which is one reason why Frank is still a pretty good golfer.

Photos D and E (above and opposite). Checking for head movement

Checking the Right Knee

Compare the right knee position in photos D and E. It has moved backward considerably, but it shouldn't. If you were to draw a line from the ball through Frank's left shoulder, you would see a really flat swing with the hands way below where they should be. Obviously, the years have taken their toll, and when Frank saw these pictures he couldn't believe how flat his swing had become.

However, the good points of his swing are still there—the head position, the club face square at the top of his backswing, and a good hip turn.

The baseline (AA), the line perpendicular to it (BB), and the diagonal (CC) are all drawn on another pair of prints (see photos F and G). Can you spot the additional fault? It's head movement. My head has moved forward two inches at the top of the backswing, and unless I'm lucky I'm going to hit behind the ball on the swing. But my right knee position is good.

Photos F and G (above and opposite). Checking for head movement

Swinging in the Barrel

Percy Boomer's classic *On Learning Golf*, published in 1946, first used the idea of "swinging inside a barrel" to describe what happens to your hips during the golf swing. Many teachers still use Boomer's idea without knowing its source. You can make a photographic check of your own hip action that will quickly show whether you are still "inside the barrel" when you finish your swing. If you aren't, you will not play better golf until you correct the situation.

The routine is similar to the one used in checking the shoulder turn, except the pictures are taken from a point directly in back of you (with the photographer directly in back of you, his back to the sun). Again, use a tripod or brace the camera.

Assume your address position. Have picture Number 1 taken. Go to the top of your backswing and stop. Take picture Number 2. Complete the swing and stop. Take picture Number 3.

When you have the three prints in front of you, take the address print (photo H) and draw a horizontal line (AA) through your heels. Perpendicular to line AA, draw a line (BB) along the right hip to line AA, then draw a line (CC) parallel to BB along the left hip.

On the backswing (photo I) draw in the same heel line. Measure how far the perpendicular lines (AA and BB) are from the edge of photo H and repeat them exactly in photo I. At the top of the backswing, note that the right hip has turned away without touching line BB.

On the follow-through (photo J) repeat the same process. Note how the left hip is still touching line CC. If it had moved beyond that line, my swing would be out of position.

Photo H. Checking the hip turn—1

Photo I. Checking the hip turn—2

Photo J. Checking the hip turn—3

5

Special Swing Thoughts for Seniors

As we seniors grow older, we tend to become shorter (an average of ½ inch per decade), probably heavier, and certainly broader than we were at forty. These changes have their effect on both your address position and swing, developed from earlier years with a different body build.

For a senior to stop going downhill, it is necessary not only to stretch those old golfing muscles but also to make swing adjustments. Don't try to make all these swing adjustments at one time, however. Your present swing took years to put together. If you make too many changes at once, your game (and you) will fall apart.

You know as well as I what too much thinking about swing mechanics can do to any golf shot. Bob Toski calls it "paralysis by analysis." For one thing, forcing yourself to assume a new position, however small the change, requires unused muscles to come into action. This will naturally feel awkward at first. But if you've done the stretching exercises described in Chapter 2, the required adjustments outlined below will not be difficult.

The Grip

Years ago Harry Vardon developed what is generally considered the most effective grip, the overlapping grip. Most golfers believe that because they overlap the little finger of the right hand, they are holding the club the way Vardon did. This is only part of the story. In photo K, the Vardon Grip is shown in a bronze replica of Vardon's hands, one of my most prized golf trophies.

Photographs L and M show the positioning of the little finger and the thumb of the right hand. Notice how the fingers are actually separated from each other (photo N), rather than being held tightly together. The only way you can achieve this finger separation is to bend the first finger of either hand at the first joint, not at the knuckle.

If you take your grip this way, your right little finger will position itself much like Vardon's, as will your right thumb. By forming your grip this way, you'll be a lot less "wristy," having much better control. When you first try it, though, be careful not to tighten at the elbows.

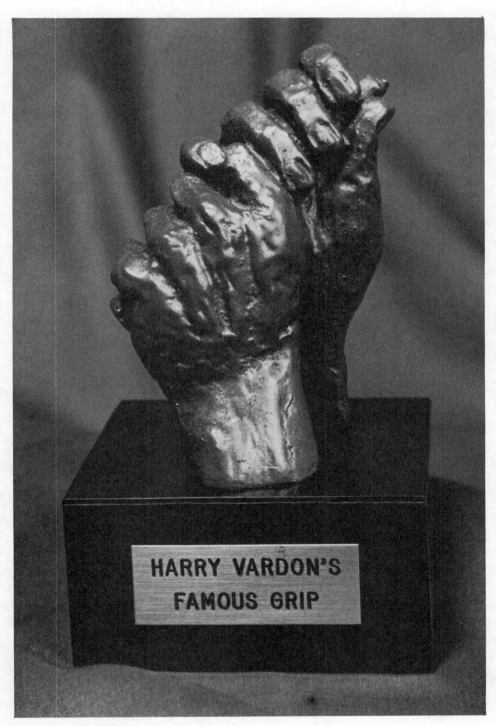

Photo K. The Vardon Grip

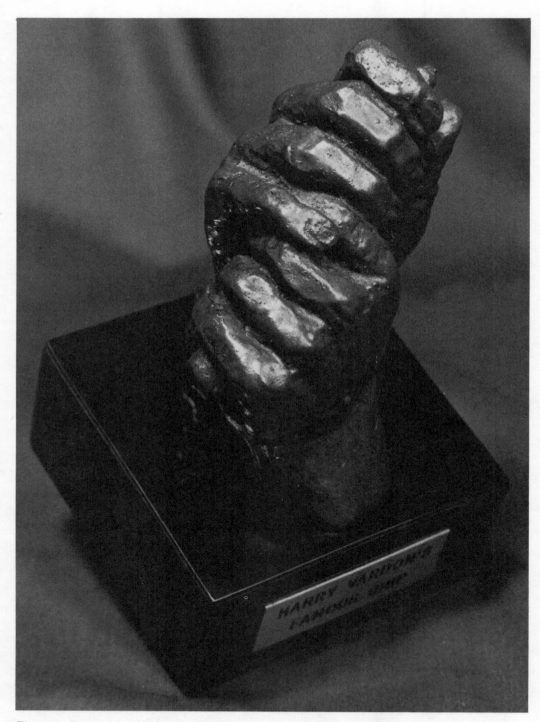

Photo L. The Vardon Grip: note the position of the right little finger

Photo M. The Vardon Grip: note the position of the right thumb

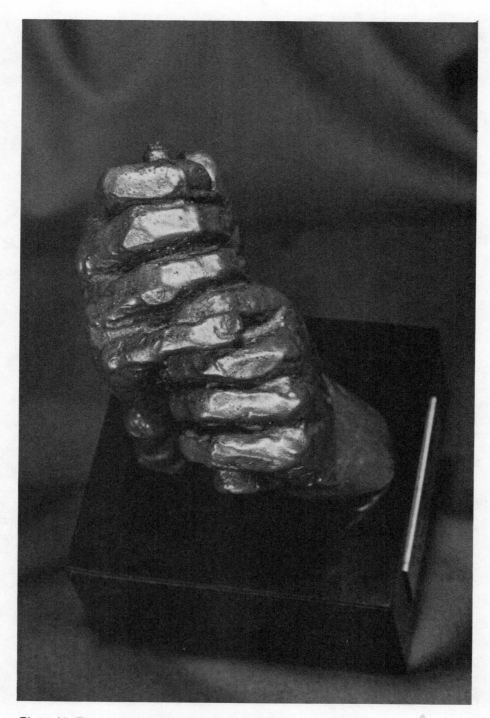

Photo N. The Vardon Grip: note the separation of the fingers

Hands come in all different shapes and sizes. Through experience, plus what the experts have written, we know that the golf club should not be held with a viselike grip. If you are gripping and swinging properly, if you have stretched your shoulder and arm muscles sufficiently, you should be able to feel your club at the top of your swing. If not, the beast in you has taken over. You will inevitably tighten up at the top of your swing, and that means you will probably not get a good hit.

This story is told about Vardon when he was paired with a new member at his home club, much to his dislike. The new member was a hacker, and during the game he lost six balls. Taciturn as always, Vardon had not said a word to his playing partner during the round, trying instead to concentrate on his own game.

Finally, the new member said, "I'm sorry, Mr. Vardon, but I have lost all my golf balls. Could you loan me one?"

Vardon, known for always hitting the ball dead straight, replied, "Sir, I only carry one ball."

Compare your own grip with Vardon's. It's a great opportunity to get a grip lesson right from the source.

One solution to the grip pressure problem is, when addressing the ball, to grab the club with all your might, hold it tight for a second, then relax your grip. You will now have the right grip pressure for your swing. Just be sure that you use no greater pressure at the top of your backswing.

In my own case, after checking my grip against Vardon's, I found I was not carrying the club as much in the fingers of the right hand as he did. Adjusting, I was less tempted to power the ball from the top of the swing, felt less urgency about getting the club started down.

The Width of the Stance

How far apart should the feet be when taking a stance? The usual answer is about shoulder width. This may or may not be the right answer, and there is a simple way of finding out.

1. Grip your driver normally and place it directly on the ground in front of you with your feet together.

2. Raise the driver shoulder height and parallel to the ground, straight out in front of you.

3. Widen your stance so your weight is on the inside of both feet. Both knees will flex and point in.

This is the proper width for you. But it has been arrived at by an intuitive sense of balance, not by placing the feet where you think they should be placed.

In a golf swing, your weight shifts to the right on the backswing, to the left on the forward swing. When you were a toddler, you learned to balance your weight and keep it balanced as you moved. You never lose that balancing ability.

In this check you have supported your body weight and the weight of the club equally on both feet, which have moved the proper distance apart for the best balance with minimum effort.

You can easily find if there is any difference between your normal stance width and what this test shows. Take a normal stance with a driver and place a tee in front of each toe. Then perform the width check and see if there is any difference. For the record, my stance was two inches narrower than it should have been, and my play immediately improved as soon as I made the two-inch adjustment. Because I was properly balanced, my knees moved much more freely on the downswing. It is such a little point, but it can make a great difference.

The Arms at Address

Just as your stance needs checking, so does your arm position at address. How you position them may be correct. Then again, some small changes may be in order. This check should not be tried until you have been stretching regularly and are able to make a good, full shoulder turn.

1. Take your regular address position with your driver.

2. Go to the top of your backswing and stop.

3. Your left arm should be above your right arm. The back of your left wrist should be a straight-line continuation of your left forearm.

4. Keeping your left arm above your right arm, return to the address position with the back of your left wrist pointing skyward.

5. Square your wrists as you do at impact.

Now your arms are positioned as they should be when you address the ball. You have always known that the address and impact positions of your arms should be as similar as possible. Make whatever adjustments are necessary in your address position.

In my case both elbows were out of position at address, so whenever I hit a good shot I had to compensate for a poor address setup. Small wonder that when I hit a wedge I never knew on which side of the flag the ball would wind up, much less how far away. There was a time when I could always get within fifteen feet of the green from seventy yards with no sweat, but I lost that ability because of my poor arm position at address. I never knew why until I came up with this arm position check.

How to Get More Feel into Your Golf Swing

Golf has been described as a game of relaxation. In my opinion, it's not so much a matter of relaxation as it is of not tightening up at the wrong time. A golf club accelerates to around one hundred miles per hour in the hitting area, so if your hands are completely relaxed you stand a good chance of losing your club, maybe the rest of your foursome as well.

On the other hand, if you grip the club at the top of your backswing with the same strength used in the hitting area you are dead before you start. As we get older, our reflexes slow down, which means we tend to tighten our muscles too soon, thereby losing smoothness and rhythm.

Instead of being called a game of relaxation, golf ought to be described as a game of feel. If at the top of your backswing your grip is like iron, you can't feel anything. On the other hand, if everything is completely relaxed

something will probably collapse before you hit the ball. There is, of course, a middle ground. And here's a good way to find it.

1. Take your stance with a driver.

2. Go to the top of your backswing and stop.

3. Wherever you feel tension, relax. If the grip is too tight, let it out a notch. Then relax the elbows, shoulders, neck, hips, and, above all, the knees. If one side is more tense than the other, make the necessary adjustments.

4. The only tension you should feel now is in the muscles that run across your upper back below the shoulders.

One practice routine that can work wonders—from the drive to the putt—is to go to the top of your backswing and stop. Feel the tension across your back muscles, but nowhere else. Then, remembering how that felt, address the ball with the same feeling and let it fly. It will.

Square-to-Square Swing

The basic idea behind the square-to-square swing is to address the ball with the back of your left wrist and forearm and your club face all pointing toward the target.

At the top of the backswing there should be no out-of-position roll of the left wrist (although there is, of course, a roll of the left forearm, without which a backswing cannot be made). The left forearm and wrist and club face remain in the same line as they were at address. At impact, the same relationship is maintained with all three areas pointing to the target just as they did at address. This is an extremely efficient method of swinging, because no compensations are necessary on the downswing.

If the club face is closed at the top (parallel to the ground), it must be opened on the way down for a square impact. If the club face is open at the top (facing the sky), it must be closed on the way down for a square impact. The square position is halfway between.

While a great deal has been written about the advantages of the square-to-square swing, the other positions have some points in their favor, too. Lee Trevino is closed at the top, which creates a draw on the ball and can produce greater distance, although a duck hook can often result.

My own feeling is that whatever position a senior is most comfortable with at the top of his swing, no great dividends can be derived from changing. There are other areas to look at that can produce a greater return. After all, we're not preparing for the tour. All we are really trying to do is have more fun by playing better golf.

Distance and the Underhand Hit

Whether impact is called a *sweep* or a *hit*, it is still the moment of contact between the club head traveling around one hundred miles per hour and a stationary ball. My advice to seniors is to keep the left arm above the right arm at impact. It's the same motion as an underhanded bounce pass with a basketball. It's important that every effort be made to

prevent any lowering of the left upper arm at impact. In my opinion, failure to do this is one of the paramount reasons why seniors lose their distance. Due to loss of height, we unconsciously tend to compensate by breaking the left elbow at address more than we should. Just telling someone to straighten his left arm more at address, however, is not enough. But when the arms are positioned at address by the method I've described earlier for positioning them at the top of the swing, the "bounce pass" arm position is secured.

You cannot correct a golf swing by adjusting one part without that adjustment relating to the other parts. If the image of the underhand basketball toss is kept in mind for the impact position, the left arm will be reasonably straight and will still be over the right arm in the follow-through. Other parts, like the wrists and the right arm, should fall into their positions automatically.

Fortunately, the ability to square the wrists

Figure 32. Underhand hit

at impact, while the arms are in the underhand hit position, never leaves us, no matter how old we get. It's strictly a reflex action. Moreover, this same position should be maintained as long as possible on the followthrough. It's the key to distance. Work on it. It can add length with no effort.

Swing and Cock, or Cock and Swing?

During the backswing, the left arm moves over and above the right arm into the "bounce pass" hit position. Most senior golfers will be more consistent if their wrists are fully cocked by the time their arms are about waist high.

Normally, the automatic wrist cock is caused by the weight of the club at the top of the backswing. For a senior, this method puts strain on the left wrist and makes it more difficult to keep the wrist lined up with the left forearm. But with the wrists cocked as the arms reach waist high, there is no further strain on the left wrist at the top. If it is properly aligned halfway back, it will stay that way. Half shots are also made much easier using this method.

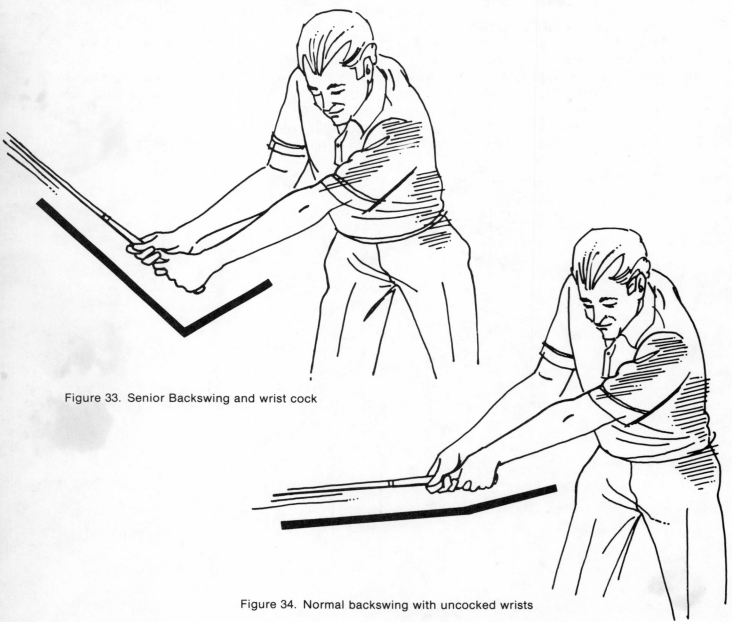

Figure 33. Senior Backswing and wrist cock

Figure 34. Normal backswing with uncocked wrists

Starting the Swing

While a great deal can be done to improve your reflexes with the exercise program in Chapter 2, they will never be as good as they once were. The concept of a one-piece swing, with everything beginning at the same time, is still as valid as it always was—if you can still do it. But many seniors lose the feel of the one-piece action, and horrible shots result. If this happens, try starting your backswing with your hip turn. I find this the best way to get it all going together again.

Being Consistent

Consistency eludes many golfers. So many factors are involved that it's often a case of not seeing the forest for the trees. Because of a loss of reflexes, small things can happen that go unnoticed.

The next time you address the ball, imagine there is a pole extending from the tip of your chin straight down to the ground. Stay behind this pole during your backswing, and be sure you don't move up on it in the downswing. If you point your chin to the right at address, the pole system works even better.

Lacking perception, seniors are inclined to too much movement on the downswing, so staying behind the pole will make you a far more consistent golfer. This also works well in putting.

Figure 35. Being consistent

What to Think about When Playing

When you swing a golf club, you have time for only two thoughts. The first comes from watching Bob Toski. Once in a while, as he takes his stance, Bob will move his club back slowly, tracing the path of his backswing perhaps a third of the way back. He doesn't do this every time, and neither should you. But it's a great way to remind yourself of the proper way to start a good swing. If you are trying to improve your game, trace the beginning and lower part of your backswing by holding the club with the left hand only. Don't make a big deal out of it, but from time to time trace the path you want your club head to take as it goes back—low to the ground and inside the line of flight. Your first thought on swinging the club, therefore, is to make sure the club head is following the path you have picked out for it.

The second thought comes at the top of the backswing. When you have made your shoulder turn and your body is coiled, the downswing becomes a reflex. But it is not a nonthought period unless you are completely tight at the top. The one thought must be: move the knees. I hate the use of the word "drive" to describe this action, because that seems much too violent. And violence at this point brings in all kinds of unnecessary movements. But you must begin the forward motion of your knees at this point.

In summation, here are the special swing thoughts every senior should remember as he seeks to improve his game:

1. Study the Vardon grip and utilize this technique as much as possible.

2. Check your stance to make sure you are in proper balance.

3. Check your arm position at address. Make sure your left arm (if you're a right-hander) is above your right arm.

4. Golf is a game of feel, not relaxation. The only tension you should feel at the top of your backswing is in the muscles that run across your upper back below the shoulders.

5. The square-to-square swing is fine, but don't change a comfortable swing just to accommodate it.

6. Use the "bounce pass" technique to secure the proper arm position in the downswing.

7. Cock your wrists early, when your arms are waist high.

8. For consistency, imagine a pole extending from your chin to the ground. Stay behind it.

9. Restrict your thoughts during the swing to just two. Trace the path you want the club head to follow at the start of the backswing, and begin forward motion of your knees at the start of the downswing.

10. To insure a one-piece swing, start the backswing with a hip turn.

6

From Tee to Green

As we age, of course, most of our physical abilities diminish. The senior golfer should notice it first in his reflexes. The smooth-flowing backswing, once just a matter of routine, is no longer easy. Each year, your handicap inches upward. Some of the suggestions that follow will, I hope, make your swing flow as smoothly as it used to.

Putting

Golfers tell a story about Glenna Collett and Patty Berg, at that time a sixteen-year-old child prodigy. Glenna was the reigning queen of golf and some years ahead of Patty. Supposedly they were playing for the United States Golf Association Ladies' title and Patty was knocking in ten- and fifteen-footers. Toward the end of the match, Glenna remarked, "Someday that little girl is going to find out what a hard thing that is to do."

Putting is the game within the game. It's the great equalizer. It makes strong men cry, small men heroes. The difference lies in a radius five feet from the flag.

It's a little like pitching pennies—a completely reflex action, which, after two or three tries, anyone knows what it takes to win. The same is true in putting. A rank beginner, after getting used to hitting the ball, can putt within two or three feet of the hole almost every time. Even a hacker can knock a fifty- or sixty-footer to within three feet of the pin and never think twice about it. You hardly see anyone—male, female, young, old—leave a sixty-footer halfway. So speed is not the problem.

The problem is that putting gets more difficult the closer you get to the hole. If almost anyone can put the ball within three feet of the hole from sixty feet, you'd think it would be simple enough to knock it in from three feet. Not so.

Watch someone practice his putting the next time you're on the practice green. They usually drop three balls on the ground and knock them to the hole one after the other without changing stance. Granted, putting is a combination of speed and direction, but hitting three balls from the same place practices only speed. Practicing the line, far more important, can only be done by walking away after each tap and setting up again.

Long putting is not the problem. The second putt—getting the ball into the hole from close by—is the tough part. Most golfers have developed their own putting style, one they're comfortable with. Trouble begins when you set up all putts, long and short, the same way.

Think about it. You rarely find anyone knocking a three-footer three feet past the cup. And you seldom find anyone leaving a three-footer short. Usually the ball runs six to eight inches past the cup—meaning that the distance is right, the direction wrong.

Speed is not a problem, because it is completely instinctive. You can prove this to yourself by standing fifteen feet from the hole and putting two balls, one with a six-inch backswing, one with a twelve-inch backswing. Both will go about the same distance, because you know by instinct how hard to hit.

The key to putting, therefore, is proper direction on short putts. Here's how to go about improving your performance on short putts. First, forget how you usually stand to the ball. Forget the placement of your feet and the line of your shoulders. Forget everything about stance. Simply step up to the ball, rest the putter head directly behind the ball, and aim at the cup, making sure that the shaft is at a right angle to the line, holding the putter lightly between the thumb and forefinger of your left hand.

Now take your usual grip and stand wherever comfortable, so you can move the putter a few inches back from the ball and then hit it on the same line. The method works, because it emphasizes direction.

So, when you practice your putts, concentrate on the three-footers. After you've made a practice putt, walk away before trying the next. Take a completely new stance. Hitting practice putts from the same setup position practices speed. Hitting putts in a different setup position each time practices direction.

On putts that must be aimed outside the cup, just sighting the line and putting away usually causes one to overcorrect. Most seniors will get a better line if they first line up the putt square to the hole, regardless of borrow, and then make whatever necessary adjustment for the borrow.

A golf cup is approximately three golf balls in diameter. On a short putt, assuming no break, aiming for the midpoint will give the ball a chance to go in, even if it is off from the center of the cup.

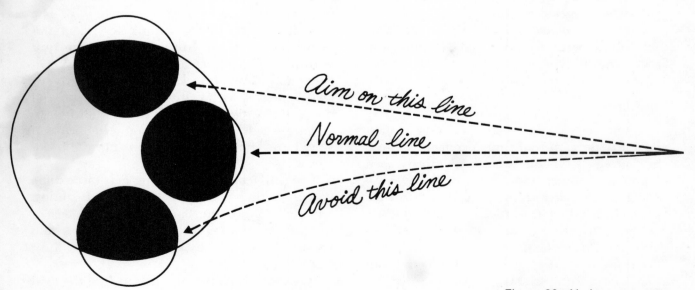

Figure 36. Aiming your putts

When a putt is missed, nine times out of ten it is missed on the left side of the cup (assuming you are right-handed).

A good crap shooter always makes his bets to lower the odds against him. You can do the same on short putts by aiming one golf ball to the right of your normal aiming line. This means that a putt hit straight will go in, but it also means that a putt hit with a slight hook will go in. The chances of your hitting a putt off line to the right side are minimal.

So try this the next time you play and see if you don't knock in more than three-footers. And use the same strategy when taking aim on breaking putts. Always make your aiming point one golf-ball width to the right of the center line.

Some seniors get the yips on short putts. This can be as terrifying as shanking, because you never know when it's going to happen. The yips are a result of an uncontrollable, viselike grip at the beginning of the downswing. The backswing is fine, but the right hand grabs on the downswing.

The best way to avoid this is to form your grip, putting both hands together, before taking the club. Then hold the putter with as light a grip as possible. Another tip is, after forming your grip, to apply pressure from the thumb pad of the right hand against the thumb pad of the left hand, still keeping a light grip. This will work for you even if you're on the eighteenth hole with a three-footer for a win and a large gallery watching. You may have the yips, but they won't ruin your swing if you use the right thumb pad for more togetherness. Remember, when you need courage, press the right thumb pad hard against the left thumb pad.

Alignment Problems

Many seniors have in-and-out problems when lining up their shots. They walk up to the ball from behind, form their grip, place the club behind the ball, and put both feet in proper position.

If everything falls into place correctly, the shoulders should be parallel to the target line, along with the hips, knees, and toes. If they are not, there's a good chance of a mishit. Often a senior thinks his alignment is correct, but it isn't. The problem is usually with the hips, which tend to open. Again, this is a result of changed body measurements without making the necessary compensations. If you are two inches shorter than you used to be, the most natural thing is to crouch a little, making it easy to open the hips. Worse, this position feels completely comfortable. Even the left leg can be aimed away from the line without your realizing it.

An easy way to fix alignment is to change the order of taking your stance. Don't form your grip first. Instead, position the club, holding it lightly between the thumb and forefinger of the left hand. Make sure the club face is on target and the shaft is at a right angle to the hitting angle. Set up in the usual way, but form your grip at the last part of the act, not the first.

This method helps bring everything square naturally. When Frank Stranahan toured, he always took his stance this way. Henry Russell, one of Florida's top senior golfers and former head of the U.S.G.A. Greens Section, also uses it. Believe me, it works.

Hitting a High or Low Ball

If you wanted to throw a baseball over a tree, you'd tilt your shoulders back at the end of your windup, so the throw would go high into the air. To hit a golf ball high you do the same thing, only you do it at address. The tilt will cause you to place the club a little farther forward than you normally do. But telling someone to address the ball forward from the normal position conveys only part of the story.

When you angle your shoulders for a high shot, your hands automatically go slightly behind the ball, which makes it natural to play the ball an inch or two more forward than normal. Conversely, for a low shot you want your shoulder line parallel to the ground. The hands then move ahead of the ball, addressed several inches behind the normal position. It all falls into place naturally from the tilt of the shoulders.

Figure 37. High shot

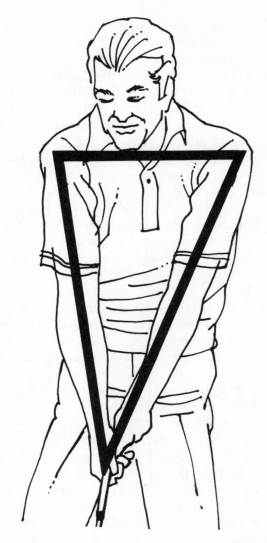

Figure 38. Low shot

It's not enough, however, simply to address the ball several inches farther back. But if you control the flight of the ball by the set of your shoulders, the other adjustments will come naturally.

Hitting a Draw or a Fade

To draw the ball, line yourself up about ten yards to the right of your normal target. Your shoulders, hips, knees, and feet should all be aimed at this line. Just how much to the right is a matter of judgment, but it should not be too much or the draw will turn into a hook.

When you are aligned properly, aim your club face on the real target without changing your grip or anything else in your swing.

Swing just the same as you normally would, and the ball will draw.

To hit a fade, line up about ten yards to the left of the target, again making sure that your shoulders, hips, knees, and feet are all on this line. Aim your club face at the desired target and take your normal swing. The ball will fade.

Deliberate hooks and slices are just more of the same. They are draws or fades on a larger scale. They should be part of every golfer's bag of tricks, because they are easy to do and are stroke savers when you have to scramble.

Forward Press or Standing Start

Since the Bobby Jones era, a forward press

has been considered essential for the start of any golf swing. It's simply a slight leftward turn of the hips, with or without a flexing of the wrists, and is a good way of freeing tight muscles. Some golfers also use it to rehearse the timing of their swing.

Though the forward press is still used by many top golfers, it is not nearly as conspicuous as it used to be. A standing start may feel more comfortable for a senior, but a forward press will add consistency.

The modern forward press is almost invisible—a slight weight transfer to the left, back to the right, again slightly to the left before going into the backswing. It's worthwhile to try as a swing loosener.

Another motion many good golfers use at address is to raise the club, perhaps an inch or two, two or three times before starting back. This movement is in response to an inconspicuous cocking and uncocking of the wrists. But it should involve only the wrists, not the arms.

Trap Shots

Trap shots are supposed to be easy, but for years I didn't believe it. Many people go through their entire golfing life with "trap terror" in their innards.

Once I served as an official of the rules committee of the U.S.G.A. Open at the Congressional Country Club in Washington, D.C. That was the year Ken Venturi won. The hole, a long par four, had a slight left dogleg, wide open on the drive but with a second shot to an abruptly elevated green. A trap ran just in front of the right half of the green, another all along the green on the left side. If the second shot was slightly off to the right or short, it was trapped. The left-side trap along the side of the green did not come into play nearly as often, so a shot just short on the left was usually not penalized.

Of those players who did not hit the green, more than half of them wound up in the sand, and most of the others were left with a short chip. After watching play all day, there was no question in my mind that the pros could get closer to the pin from the sand than they could with an ordinary short chip. One reason could be that they practice the trap shot more. The other reason is perhaps because it is an easier shot.

The main reason the ordinary golfer has trouble getting out of sand is simple. He does not adjust his shoulders the same as if he were going to hit the ball over a tree. If the sand shot is played without shoulder adjustment, there is no way it can come off.

The other usual adjustments—a weaker grip with the left hand, opening the club face to cut the shot, opening the stance—may add finesse, but the way to make the shot come off every time is to imagine you are cutting it over a high fence.

Estimating Distances

The best way to estimate distance is to pace off fifty yards between two objects, then fix this distance in your mind as a reference. Then, when you are on an unfamiliar course without markers, you can estimate distances by figuring how many of these fifty-yard spans are between you and the flag.

To check yourself, try it a few times, then pace off the actual distance. The checkoff is easy and works quite well.

The Countdown

Once in your life all it took was a forward press and—boom!—you were set to go. But as a senior golfer, making a countdown before each shot, from a drive to a putt, can be a great help.

The first point in the countdown is alignment. The lowest part of everyone's swing is opposite the left armpit, and this part of the swing must be perpendicular to an imaginary line drawn from the ball to the target. Many golfers, whose right eye is the lead eye, position themselves from the right shoulder; worse, they leave positioning to instinct. A good golfer will always make an alignment check from his *left* shoulder (assuming right-handedness) as he is getting into position.

Other checkpoints follow: Relax the hands, elbows, shoulders, neck, hips, and, last of all, knees. Make a conscious effort to relax one point after another until nothing is tight—the countdown. Once all systems are go, let it fly.

Equipment

A senior, lacking the flexibility and strength he once had, can compensate by using clubs with a lesser swing weight and a softer shaft. This is true—*if* you do not follow the exercise program recommended in Chapter 2. Nonexercising seniors should probably use a C-9 swing weight and shafts with greater flex.

But if you've followed my program, you should be able to handle your regular clubs without any problems. Today I hit the ball as far as ever. I won't hit many par fives in two, but then I never did. However, if a par five is in the 460-475-yard range, I can sometimes get it home. There are not many of these short par fives around today, however.

I never was comfortable using one hundred compression balls. It always felt as if I were hitting a rock. The same was true whenever I used a club with a D-5 swing weight and a stiff shaft. This is purely a personal reaction, of course, and I'm sure I could have adjusted to both the high-compression ball and heavier clubs. But I could never see any great advantage to this. My clubs were always D-1 with regular shafts and seemed to suit me. Perhaps the heavier swing weight would have given me more distance, but how much? For a few additional yards, there's really no great advantage, in my view.

A five wood is the equivalent of a three iron as far as distance is concerned, but the trajectory of the ball, being much higher, gives it a softer landing with less run. Many seniors find the five wood easier to control, so they carry it rather than a two wood.

Some good seniors go even further. Frank Strafaci carries a six wood instead of a four iron and a seven wood instead of a five iron. Of course, Frank's swing, always on the flat side, has become even flatter as he has grown older. Run an imaginary line between the ball and the center of Frank's shoulder (see page 69, photo E) and you will see what I mean. Now you can understand why he has more success with six and seven woods than with irons. He is so flat that his iron shots to the green hit too low for accuracy, hooking too often. Frank is still a very good player, don't get me wrong, but when the pressure is turned on he can duck hook like a teenager.

Playing with the woods helps him, and many other senior golfers, overcome this problem.

Epilogue

After doing the routines in this book every day for several years now, I am hardly a basket case. I am not quite as good a golfer as I would like, but then no one is. That's part of the fascination of golf, whether you have a handicap of twenty or play from scratch.

A friend once said that when you are born, there's a number tattooed on your left shoulder—your handicap. And it makes no difference how hard you try, that's your number. There is no truth in this statement, of course. You can always get better if you work at it.

Today, when I tee it up, I am not afraid of making an idiot of myself. I feel the top of my backswing, my shoulders are not rigid, and I make a good turn and finish. It's the result of stretching and diet supplementation. They are equally important, complementing each other.

There are a few points stressed here worth repeating. When you start the stretching rou-

tines, don't try to improve your game until most of the kinks are worked out. The stretches should be done easily, without burning. There is little point in trying a full golf swing if some of the shoulder and neck muscles still sting when you stretch them. When you are able to make an unrestricted, full shoulder turn without a golf club, then is the time to go to the practice tee—not before.

The more limber you make your body, the easier it becomes to swing a golf club properly. If you look around the locker room at the various pot bellies, you will see how essential it is to get the torso area under control.

A standard life-insurance table of desirable weights is not inflexible, but does provide a guideline as to what you should probably weigh, assuming you have no health problems (see table 2).

Aging, we no longer need the same number of calories required at maturity. Nature does a fairly good job of diminishing your appetite through a brain mechanism. Although not fully understood, this mechanism regulates the appetite, just as a thermostat regulates temperature. Each of us consumes roughly 12½ tons of food during a ten-year period. If this regulator were off 1 percent it would mean we'd each gain at least 125 pounds; so it is a pretty good control mechanism. Even with obese persons, the regulator is probably off no more than .03 percent.

Many of us dull the sensitivity of this mechanism by having a few martinis before dinner. A drink before dinner stimulates the appetite, so if you should lose a few pounds, remember that each drink costs you 100 calories, and to lose one pound requires a diminished intake of 3,000 calories. One drink less per day for a month will help you lose that pound. Actually, you'll probably lose more, because the desire for seconds at the dining table will diminish.

Another easy way to lose a few pounds is simply to cut bread and butter from your diet, and use less sugar. Unless something is wrong healthwise, losing a few pounds and keeping them off is not too difficult. Obviously, if you do not have to swing around a protruding belly, golf is an easier game.

Using vitamins C and E, a vitamin supplement, and bran to increase fiber in your diet may alleviate some of the effects of aging as well as improve your golf game. This is not to say you will stop aging. It simply means that some of the symptoms of aging can probably be held back.

Science holds that something has been proven when a performance under similar circumstances can be repeated innumerable times with the same result. Here, the only real proof is: Does it work for you? Your own reaction to the program, after trying it several months, is the only proof. That someone rec-

TABLE 2. DESIRABLE WEIGHTS FOR MEN OF AGES 25 AND OVER*

Weight in Pounds According to Frame (Indoor Clothing)

Height: (with shoes on) 1-inch heels		Small Frame	Medium Frame	Large Frame
Feet	Inches			
5	2	112-120	118-120	126-141
5	3	115-123	121-133	129-144
5	4	118-126	124-136	132-148
5	5	121-129	127-139	135-152
5	6	124-133	130-143	138-156
5	7	128-137	134-147	142-161
5	8	132-141	138-152	147-166
5	9	136-145	142-156	151-170
5	10	140-150	146-160	155-174
5	11	144-154	150-165	159-179
6	0	148-158	154-170	164-184
6	1	152-162	158-175	168-189
6	2	156-167	162-180	173-194
6	3	160-171	167-185	178-199
6	4	164-175	172-190	182-204

*Metropolitan Life Insurance Company, New York

ommends it or does not recommend it is valid only if that person has tried it. And then his conclusion is valid only for him. This is a personal matter in which only you can be the judge.

Coincidentally, I was taking vitamins C and E before Dr. Pauling published his work on vitamin C and before Dr. Stone published *The Healing Factor,* bringing up to date the vast research that had been done on vitamin C. This was several years before the connection between them and aging was publicized. For me they have worked wonders.

As for exercise, to be against it is like being against motherhood. The trouble is, exercise for most of us is plain boring. Only when it is tied to something like improving your golf game is there an incentive for daily continuance. Even then, at times you will feel like skipping it.

If you let yourself go for a week without stretching, you will be reminded by the back-sliding of your golf game and by the way you react when you do stretch again. Even without missing a day there will be times when new spasms appear in areas completely free from trouble the day before. The older you are, the more this will happen.

Remember that a good finish is the result of a good swing. Have a picture taken of your finish after hitting a ball on the practice tee. Depending on what it shows, work on it. It will tell a lot of the story.

I can only hope you will derive as much benefit as I have from the stretching exercises and diet supplementation. Not only will your golf game improve, but you will have some of those extra dividends, as I did, to show for your efforts. Life will be much more fun in every way. And that's what we all want, isn't it?

Sources

This selected reading list will be of interest to those wanting to go into the subjects of nutrition and aging more thoroughly. To begin with, I would single out *Prolongevity*, by Albert Rosenfeld, and *Nutrition Against Disease,* by Dr. Roger J. Williams.

Prolongevity is an excellent update of all the current biochemical research and theories on aging by the former science editor of *Life* magazine.

Nutrition Against Disease is by a former president of the American Chemical Society who discovered and synthesized pantothenic acid, a B vitamin. The chapter called "How Can We Delay Old Age?" should be of interest to any reader of this book.

Nutrition in a Nutshell, also by Dr. Williams, is an important update on nutritional research.

Vitamin E and Aging, Erwin D. Cyan, suggests some ways to provide better health and perhaps a longer life.

Vitamin E—the Key to a Healthy Heart, Herbert Bailey, represents the author's personal experiences with vitamin E in overcoming the effects of a heart attack. It includes a chapter on E. P. Taylor's use of vitamin E on his thoroughbred racehorses in 1958 and 1959.

The Healing Factor, Dr. Irwin Stone, is an important and impressive work that assembles relevant documents and puts in perspective the massive amount of research on vitamin C. The chapter on aging is of interest.

Vitamin C, the Common Cold and the Flu, Linus Pauling, presents the author's latest evidence in a follow-up to his *Vitamin C and the Common Cold.* Most of the uproar against Dr. Pauling's theories comes from people who have never tried vitamin C themselves.

Let's Eat Right to Keep Fit is by Adelle Davis, a brilliant biochemist who has worked with physicians throughout her career. This book, originally published in 1954 and revised in 1970, is an excellent survey of the role vitamins play in nutrition.

Let's Get Well, also Adelle Davis, was published in 1965. It surveys the therapeutic use of vitamins in nutrition and documents their use for many common complaints.

Mental and Elemental Nutrients, Carl C. Pfeiffer, Ph.D., M.D., a biochemist and physician, is a physician's guide to nutrition and health care, covering the usual nutrients as well as the trace minerals.

Fundamentals of Normal Nutrition, Professor Corinne H. Robinson, is an excellent basic reference book on nutrition.

The Physiological Effects of Wheat Germ Oil on Humans in Exercise, Professor Thomas K. Cureton, gives the author's research procedures and findings covering about 900 subjects during a period of nearly two decades.

The Family Guide to Better Food and Better Health, Ronald M. Deutsch, deals with weight control and nutrition from the conventional point of view.

Freedom from Backaches, Lawrence W. Friedman, M.D., and Lawrence Galton, details the many methods that can be used to prevent and cure back complaints.

Body, Mind, and the B Vitamins, Adams and Murray, is a rundown on the B vitamins, with references to aging that are of particular interest.

Executive Health is published monthly by Richard Stauton, Post Office Box 589, Rancho Santa Fe, California 92067. Its editorial board represents a "Who's Who" of both medicine and nutrition. This journal's authoritative reports—on aging, backaches, vitamins, minerals, and medicines,—cover every area of health and reflect the current opinions of the best minds in the country.

The Search for the Perfect Swing, John Stobbs and Alistair Cochran, reveals the fundamental mechanics of the golf swing as sponsored by the Golf Society of Great Britain.

Index